Contents

The Music Around You

Did you ever get a song stuck in your head? Maybe you just couldn't help singing it out loud. Sometimes a song reminds you of a day with your friends or a fun vacation. Other times a tune may stay in your mind just because you like it so much. Listening to music can be fun and memorable for everyone.

We hear music everywhere we go. Music is played on television shows and commercials. There are even television stations dedicated to music.

Most radio stations play one type, or **genre**, of music. Some play only country music. Others play just classical music. Still others play a mixture of different kinds of rock music. Just pick a kind of music that you like, and you will find a radio station that plays it!

The different genres of music have many things in common, though. They all use instruments. Some instruments are played in many different types of music. The differences are in the ways instruments are played. For example, the drumbeats are different in various music genres.

Some kinds of music have **lyrics** that are sung by singers. Did you know that the human voice is often referred to as an instrument?

Cool HIP-HOP MUSIC

Create & Appreciate What Makes Music Great!

Karen Latchana Kenney

ABDO Publishing Company

Visit us at www.abdopublishing.com

Published by ABDO Publishing Company, 8000 West 78th Street, Edina, Minnesota 55439. Copyright © 2008 by Abdo Consulting Group, Inc. International copyrights reserved in all countries. No part of this book may be reproduced in any form without written permission from the publisher. The Checkerboard Library™ is a trademark and logo of ABDO Publishing Company.

Printed in the United States.

Design and Production: Mighty Media, Inc.
Photo Credits: Anders Hanson, Photodisc, Shutterstock
Series Editor: Pam Price

Library of Congress Cataloging-in-Publication Data

Kenney, Karen Latchana.
  Cool hip-hop music : create & appreciate what makes music great! / Karen Latchana Kenney.
     p. cm. -- (Cool music)
  Includes index.
  ISBN 978-1-59928-971-7
  1. Rap (Music)--History and criticism--Juvenile literature. 2. Rap (Music)--Instruction and study--Juvenile. I. Title.

  ML3531.K46 2008
  782.421649--dc22

                          2007040585

9/10 782.42   SGL 53916
      Ken
              $25.65

Note to Adult Helpers

Some activities in this book require the help of an adult. An adult should closely monitor any use of a sharp object, such as a utility knife, or perform that task for the child.

Playing music can be as fun as listening to it! Every person can play a part in a song. You can start with something simple, such as a tambourine. You could then work your way up to a more difficult instrument, such as a drum set. Remember, every great musician was once a beginner. It takes practice and time to learn how to play an instrument.

With music, one of the most important things is to have fun! You can dance to it, play it, or listen to it. Find your own musical style and make it your own!

A Mini Musical Glossary

classical music – a type of music from Europe that began centuries ago as the first written church music. Today it includes operas and music played by orchestras.

country music – a style of music that came from the rural parts of the southern United States. It is based on folk, gospel, and blues music.

hip-hop music – a style of music originally from New York City in which someone raps lyrics while a DJ plays or creates an instrumental track.

Latin music – a genre of music that includes several styles of music from Latin America. It is influenced by African, European, and native musical styles. Songs may be sung in Spanish, Portuguese, or Latin-based Creole.

reggae music – a type of music that came from Jamaica in the 1960s. It is based on African and Caribbean music and American rhythm and blues.

rock music – a genre of music that became popular in the 1950s. It is based on country music and rhythm-and-blues styles.

Hip-hop is not only about music. It is about a culture and a lifestyle. There are four main elements of hip-hop. They are DJing, MCing or rapping, graffiti art, and break dancing.

Hip-hop began in New York City as an **underground** movement. This means that this music was not widely known or played on the radio. However, over time it has broken into **mainstream** culture and spread around the world.

1973. DJ Kool Herc started break-beat disc jockeying at parties in the Bronx. This is when two identical records are played on two **turntables**. The DJ finds an instrumental break in a song. Then the DJ alternates between the two records to continuously play that instrumental break. This becomes the base for rap **lyrics**.

1982. Kurtis Blow became the first rapper to appear on television when he performed on *Soul Train*.

1975

1980

1975. Grandmaster Flash created new turntable techniques and began sampling. He also started partnering with MCs such as the Furious Five, a group of five rappers.

1979. Sugar Hill Records formed the Sugarhill Gang. Their song "Rapper's Delight" became a successful single. This song introduced many Americans to hip-hop music.

1982. Grandmaster Flash and the Furious Five released the hit single "The Message." This rap song has a social message about life in the Bronx ghetto. Afrika Bambaataa released "Planet Rock" which became a hip-hop classic. This album combines DJing, MCing, and a **techno** sound.

1982–1984. Several movies featuring hip-hop culture were released. *Style Wars* is a documentary that was shown on PBS, and *Wild Style* is a drama. They are both about graffiti and hip-hop culture. *Breakin'* and *Breakin' 2: Electric Boogaloo* are movies about break dancing. *Flashdance* also featured break dancing moves.

1993–1999. Several female rappers become popular. Salt-N-Pepa, Lil' Kim, Missy "Misdemeanor" Elliott, and Lauryn Hill released hit songs.

2003. Crunk artists produced some hit singles. Crunk is a type of hip-hop music that is high energy, has a heavy bass line, and has aggressively rapped lyrics. Lil John is a popular crunk musician.

1990–1999. Many gangsta rap artists released albums and became popular. Some of the most popular artists were Dr. Dre, Snoop Doggy Dogg, Notorious B.I.G., Ice-T, Tupac Shakur, and 2 Live Crew.

1985   1990   1995   2000

1988. Gangsta rap originated on the West Coast of the United States. The gangsta rap group N.W.A. released the album *Straight Outta Compton*.

1988. MTV created a rap show called *Yo! MTV Raps*. This series remained on the air until 1995.

2002. Alternative hip-hop with a socially conscious message grew popular in the hip-hop music scene. Blackalicious, Common, and Talib Kweli released hip-hop albums that fit into this category.

Hip-hop music keeps evolving. Underground hip-hop music scenes are alive in cities across the United States. Rap music tops the popular charts. It may have started in one small area in the Bronx, but hip-hop is now thriving around the world.

What Is Hip-Hop Music?

To make hip-hop music in its most basic form, just two **turntables**, a mixer, records, a DJ, and an MC are needed. It's the DJ's skills and techniques that create unique rhythms and sounds. The lyrical rhythm and ability of the MC characterize his or her rap style. How do these elements combine to create a hip-hop sound?

Hip-Hop Rhythm and Sound

Turntables are the basis of hip-hop music. Using different techniques, DJs play turntables and mixer-like instruments. DJs provide the beat and the sounds to back an MC's rap. DJ Kool Herc, Grandmaster Flash, and Grand Wizard Theodore pioneered the following turntable techniques used in hip-hop music.

backspinning – turning records backward by hand to repeat certain sounds.

cutting – moving between tracks on a record on the beat.

punch-phasing – hitting a break, which is a part of a song that accents the beat or rhythm, on one turntable while the record continues playing on the other turntable.

scratching – spinning a record back and forth while the needle is in the groove of the record.

sampling – using parts of existing songs to create a new song.

Rapping the Lyrics

The lyricist in hip-hop music is called a rapper or an MC. The rapper rhymes, or raps, the **lyrics** over a steady beat. How well the MC fits the lyrics to the beat is called his or her flow. When hip-hop music began, lyrics described the urban ghetto life of the South Bronx. As hip-hop has changed, so have the lyrics.

Gangsta rap tells stories about gang life on the West Coast. Some alternative rap speaks about social issues, such as war or politics. Rap lyrics explain many situations in life. They can be about something as simple as parents not understanding their kids. Or they can express something serious, such as life in a ghetto.

Who's Who in a Hip-Hop Group

The number of members in hip-hop groups varies. A basic group needs just one MC and one DJ. However, multiple MCs and other musicians are usually added to the group. The different members have different jobs in the group.

The DJ plays on two turntables, using records to create a beat and play samples.

The MC raps lyrics over the beat. Other MCs may add lyrics to the song.

Musicians, such as guitarists or keyboard players, may add to the music played by the DJ.

A vocalist may sing a repeating part in the song.

DJ

MC

MUSICIANS

VOCALIST

Hip-Hop Instruments

The hip-hop sound is created with just a few basic elements.

Hip-Hop Elements

two turntables

mixer

records

Additional Instruments

Sometimes hip-hop groups add live music to the tracks they play on the **turntables**. These are some of the instruments they might add.

drum kit

keyboard

electric guitar

Hip-Hop Tools

Hip-hop artists need some other tools in addition to turntables, records, and mixers. Without these tools, you wouldn't be able to hear the hip-hop sound.

Microphones. Microphones change the sounds from the lyricist and the turntables into electrical signals and feed them to the amplifiers.

Amplifiers. Amplifiers change electrical signals into loud sounds.

Hip-Hop Greats

There are many well-known hip-hop groups, rappers, and songs. Here is a list of just a few of the most popular hip-hop greats.

Groups

- Afrika Bambaataa
- Beastie Boys
- Black Eyed Peas
- Grandmaster Flash and the Furious Five
- Jurassic 5
- Outkast
- The Roots
- Run-DMC
- Salt-N-Pepa
- Wu-Tang Clan

Rappers

- 50 Cent
- Dr. Dre
- Eminem
- Ice Cube
- Jay-Z
- Kanye West
- Lil' Kim
- LL Cool J
- Ludacris
- Missy Elliot
- P. Diddy (Sean Combs)
- Queen Latifah
- Snoop Dogg
- Tupac Shakur

Songs

- "B.O.B.," by Outkast

- "Daylight," by Aesop Rock

- "The Jump Off," by Lil' Kim

- "Mama Said Knock You Out," by LL Cool J

- "The Message," by Grandmaster Flash and the Furious Five

- "Rapper's Delight," by Sugarhill Gang

- "The Real Slim Shady," by Eminem

- "UMI Says," by Mos Def

- "(You Gotta) Fight for Your Right (To Party!)," by Beastie Boys

Record Labels and Recording Studios

A record label is a company that signs, or hires, bands and then records and sells their music. The term *record label* comes from the paper labels that are pasted in the center of vinyl records. These are some important hip-hop record labels and some of the artists they have signed.

- Def Jam Recordings - signed LL Cool J, Jay-Z, Ludacris, Method Man, Lady Sovereign, and The Roots

- Sugar Hill Records - created Sugarhill Gang, signed Grandmaster Flash and Melle Mel

- Bad Boy Records - signed the Notorious B.I.G.

- Aftermath Entertainment - signed Eminem, Busta Rhymes, and 50 Cent

Music Production and Collection

Music Production

The way music is recorded makes a big difference in its final sound. The type of microphone used and where it is placed are very important. The **acoustics** in the recording room are critical.

Recording music is a difficult process. That is why hip-hop groups record in recording studios. A recording studio has professional recording equipment. It also has soundproof rooms. Studio engineers place the microphones and run the equipment.

Once the music is recorded, it needs to be worked with to bring out the best sound. This is mostly done with computer programs that help separate the sounds. This process is called mixing.

This sound engineer is using a mixing board.

Downloading Music

At one time, music could be bought only at record stores. Today you can buy music by downloading it onto your computer from a Web site. You can then put the downloaded music onto an MP3 player.

Sometimes people violate **copyright** law when they download music. Copyright law helps musicians get paid for their music. Some illegal Web sites let people download music without paying. You need to make sure you are downloading music from a legal Web site. Otherwise, you could be breaking copyright law.

It is also important that you get permission from an adult before downloading music. When you download music, you are charged a fee. Make sure an adult knows how much the music costs. And make sure an adult knows the Web site you are downloading from.

Record Collecting

Many people collect vinyl records. Music stores sell new and used records. You can also find used records at garage and estate sales. Many **audiophiles** prefer the sound of records. They believe the sound is warmer and truer than the sound of CDs.

Hip-hop DJs use parts of songs from old records to make new music. This is called sampling. DJs also play records on two **turntables** and use different techniques to produce different sounds.

Experience Hip-Hop Music

There are many ways to listen to hip-hop music. You can go to a live performance or listen to the radio. You can check out music at your local library or go to a community center or a museum.

At many libraries, you can check out CDs and DVDs for free. You can watch concerts on DVDs, cable channels, and public television. Here are just a few ways you can experience and learn about hip-hop music.

Concert Venues

Local newspapers usually list concerts. Look in the entertainment section for upcoming hip-hop concerts. If you are under 18, the **venue** may require that you attend with an adult. Hip-hop groups play at:

- community centers
- stadiums
- state fairs
- park bandstands
- art and music festivals

Community Centers, Art Programs, and Museums

Community centers, art programs, and museum exhibits are great ways to learn about hip-hop music. Some centers host hip-hop educational summits. There are not many permanent exhibits about hip-hop music in museums. But, some museums host traveling exhibits about hip-hop music for a short time. Check your local newspaper for exhibits visiting your hometown.

Experience Music Project

Seattle, WA
www.empsfm.org

This museum has an exhibit called "Yes Yes Y'all" which covers the first decade of hip-hop music.

B-Girl Be

Minneapolis, MN
www.bgirlbe.com

B-Girl Be is a four-day festival. It is held each year by Intermedia Arts in Minneapolis. It has art exhibits, workshops, and performances honoring women in hip-hop.

Elementz

Cincinnati, OH
www.natiyouthcenter.org

This community center focuses on providing hip-hop resources for kids. They have a recording and production studio and programs for hip-hop dance, DJing, and graffiti art.

Justice by Uniting in Creative Energy (J.U.i.C.E.)

Los Angeles, CA
www.rampartjuice.com

This youth hip-hop arts program meets weekly. They have workshops and programs for hip-hop dance, DJing, music production and recording, rhyme writing, and graffiti and mural art.

Experience Music Project

Be a Human BEATBOX

Beatboxing is using your mouth as an instrument. There are sounds you can make with your mouth that sound like different types of drum sounds. When you combine these sounds in a steady rhythm, you sound like you are playing a drum machine. Hip-hop musicians known for their beatboxing skills include Doug E. Fresh, Rhazel, Darren "Buffy, the Human Beat Box" Robinson, and Matisyahu. Listen to some of their music for inspiration.

Basic Sounds

There are three basic sounds to start with when you first learn to beatbox. They are:

- the classic kick drum, which will be marked as *b* here
- the hi-hat, which will be marked as *t* here
- the classic snare drum, which will be marked as *pf* here

Step 1

First, make the classic kick drum sound. This is a low *b* sound. Close your lips tightly together. Next, force the sound of the letter *b* through your lips. The tighter your lips, the better the sound will be. Try to make the *b* sound as low as your voice can go.

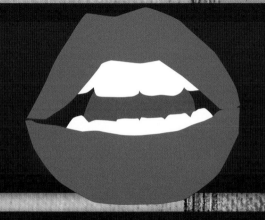

Step 2

Next, make the hi-hat sound. This is a *t* sound. Leaving your lips open, push your tongue to the top of your mouth and make a *t* sound. Do not say the letter *t*, just make the sound.

Step 3

Now, make the classic snare drum sound. This is like saying the word *poof* but without the *oo* sound. With your lips together, try saying the letters *pf* together.

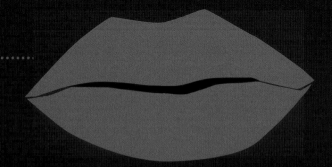

Step 4

Separately, these sounds don't seem like much. When you put them together, though, they begin to sound like drums. Try combining the sounds like this,

b-t-pf-t-b-t-pf-t

Start slowly. It's difficult to make these sounds one after the other! As you start getting better, try practicing with a **metronome** or a beat machine. That way you will know what the steady beat is. When you are even better, all you will need is your mouth to be a human beatbox!

19

Write a
RAP

Rap **lyrics** are sort of like a poem that is spoken over music. The lyrics use both rhyme and rhythm. Pick a hip-hop or a rap karaoke CD or an instrumental hip-hop track as the basis for your rap. Listen to the song you pick a few times and then start writing!

Step 1

First, pick your topic and title. These can be any subjects you like. For example, try writing about one of your favorite activities or hobbies. Then make a list of ideas you want to include in your rap lyrics.

Step 2

Now, start writing your rap. Try to make your first verse have a strong rhyming rhythm. This will set the tone for the rest of your lyrics. Try to make the last words in each pair of lines rhyme. Check out the hip-hop terms on the next page. Try to include some of these terms in your rap.

Step 3

Next, write the chorus. The chorus should be connected to your song's title and main idea. Try to make it catchy and hip sounding!

Main Idea

Going for a bike ride

Title Ideas

- cruisin'
- Bikin'
- Two miles to school
- watch the curb!

Lyric Ideas

- biking fast
- meeting up with friends
- crashing on your bike
- making your bike look good

Hip-Hop Terms

b-boy – a boy break-dancer.

b-girl – a girl break-dancer.

battle – a DJ or MC competition.

beat – the instrumental music of hip-hop.

beatbox – to create percussion sounds with your mouth.

def – excellent.

flow – how a rapper raps over the beats.

freestyle – to improvise a rap over the beats.

fresh – new or good.

old school – early hip-hop from the 1970s to the 1980s.

turntablism – playing turntables like instruments.

Step 4

Finally, rap your **lyrics** over your song. This will take some practice! Rapping is not just speaking words over a song. Experiment with how you pace and say the words. Try to make the rhythm of your lyrics match the beats in the music. Once you find the right fit, you've discovered your flow!

Do the ROBOT

Beep boop beep! I am a robot! Old school hip-hop music emphasizes loud, funky beats, booming bass lines, and weird electronic sounds. That makes it perfect for doing the robot.

Materials Needed

- stereo
- a great dance song such as "Planet Rock" by Afrika Bambaataa or "Rockit" by Herbie Hancock

The Robot Stance

The robot stance will make your other dance moves look more robotic. Stand with your feet shoulder width apart. Make sure your back is very straight, and keep your shoulders down and your neck long. Lift your arms slightly away from your body.

Next, bend your arms up at your elbows. Keep your palms open and your fingers pointing straight ahead. Remember, robots don't move their eyes, so keep your eyes straight ahead no matter which direction you move!

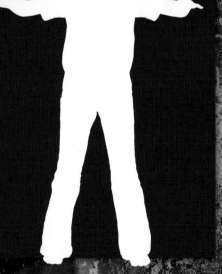

The Robot Walk

Raise one arm forward. Next, pretend that your feet are stuck to the ground. Slide one foot forward. Then, slide your other foot forward. Do not bend your knees! Keep going forward and remember to stand stiffly. Now, you are walking like a robot!

Robot Arms

Keeping your elbows bent with your fingers pointing forward, lift one arm so your hand is pointing to the ceiling. Your arm should be in an L-shape. Lower that arm and then lift and lower the other arm. Next, lift both arms at the same time.

Robot Head

Keeping your body facing forward, turn your head so you are looking to the right. When your head is turned toward the right, make sure it is slightly tipped forward. Move your head back to the center and stop quickly. Then turn your head so you are looking to the left and then back to the center. You can now look around like a robot!

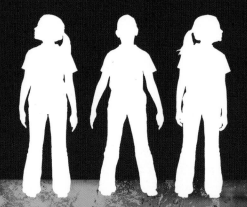

Try these movements in different combinations. Add a little bit of a bounce when you stop a movement. Try bending forward from your torso. Remember to keep your body stiff and think like a robot. Make up your own robotic moves and share them with your friends!

CLEF NOTES

The robot is only one type of break dancing. Other moves include the backspin, the caterpillar, and the moonwalk.

Sneaker ART

Materials Needed

- inexpensive canvas sneakers
- fabric markers
- scratch paper

Sneakers are a big part of hip-hop fashion. Many people who follow hip-hop culture customize their sneakers with their own art. This art is usually in a graffiti style.

Usually, this graffiti style involves thick, balloonlike lettering. Pictures and symbols such as arrows or stars are also included. Before starting this activity, be sure you have permission from an adult to customize your sneakers!

Step 1

First, make sure your canvas sneakers are clean and dry. Decide which part of the sneakers you want to customize.

Hip-Hop Name	Real Name
50 Cent	Curtis Jackson
Dr. Dre	André Young
Eminem	Marshall Mathers
Fab 5 Freddy	Fred Brathwaite
Grandmaster Flash	Joseph Sadler
Lil' Kim	Kimberly Jones
Queen Latifah	Dana Owens

Step 2

Next, choose a tag, or symbol, for yourself. This may be your initials. Or, you could make up a name for yourself. Play around with your name. For examples of hip-hop names, see the hip-hop name chart. It shows artists' stage names and their real names. Try to choose a name that says something about yourself.

Step 3

Next, practice writing your new name in different styles on a piece of scratch paper. Experiment with the letters and the colors. Find your favorite style. This is what you will draw on your sneakers.

Step 4

Finally, draw your name on your sneakers with the fabric markers. Add your favorite symbols or pictures. Make these sneakers say something about your style!

CLEF NOTES

Another way to customize your sneakers is to change your shoelaces. Try picking really wide laces or laces that are different colors. Then, experiment with the way you thread the laces through the holes.

B-Boy B-Girl
DANCE-OFF

Break dancing competitions have been around since the beginning of hip-hop. These are friendly dance competitions. A crowd gathers around an open circle of dance floor. In the middle, two dancers compete to see who has the best break dancing moves. The crowd is the judge, and their cheers tell who has won the competition.

Step 1

First, go to the library and pick out some hip-hop CDs.

Step 2

Next, set up a dance floor. Make sure you have permission from an adult. Also, make sure the area is cleared of things that could be knocked over or broken. The dance floor needs to have a smooth and flat surface, such as a garage floor. If the area does not have a smooth surface, lay out a flat piece of cardboard.

Step 3

Get your music ready. Practice a bit before the competition. Try the robot dance moves described in this book. Or check out a break dancing movie or video for some new moves.

Step 4

Now it is time for your competition! Start the music. Let your competitor dance first. When your competitor is finished with a few moves, you can take over the dance floor. Keep alternating between dancers.

Once the song is finished, ask the crowd to cheer for the dancer they thought had the best moves. Invite members of the crowd to compete as well and have lots of fun!

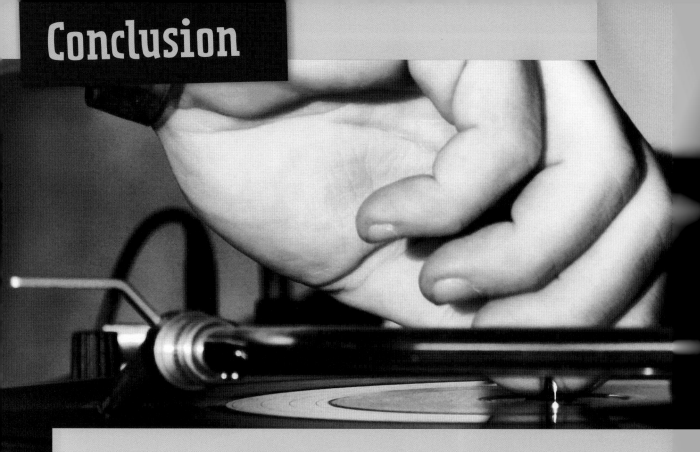

Conclusion

Hip-hop is not only about music, it is about culture and art as well. This urban culture is a great way to express your own individual style. You might try DJing, MCing, graffiti art, or break dancing.

While graffiti art is colorful and cool, it is important that it be done in a legal area. Many hip-hop youth centers have special areas where young artists can express their graffiti style. Writing a rap is something anyone can try. If you can write a rhyme, you can write your first rap! Try to express something about yourself or your life in your **lyrics**.

Many places offer hip-hop dance classes. Try one of these classes to develop your break dancing skills. Also, some youth centers have **turntables** for young people to try out their DJing abilities.

If you are collecting hip-hop music, there are many styles to choose from. You might like old school, gangsta rap, crunk, or alternative rap.

Having fun with hip-hop is not hard to do! There are always fresh beats to rock your own hip-hop style!

Glossary

acoustics – the properties of a room that affect how sound is heard in it.

audiophile – a person who is very enthusiastic about listening to recorded music.

copyright – the legal right to copy, sell, publish, or distribute the work of a writer, musician, or artist.

genre – a category of art, music, or literature.

lyrics – the words of a song.

mainstream – representing the tastes, thoughts, or values of a large segment of a society or group.

metronome – a device that marks time or rhythm with a regular ticking sound.

techno – a style of dance music that features a fast beat and no lyrics. It is usually made with synthesizers.

turntable – the round, rotating platform on which records are placed; a record player.

underground – published or produced by those on the leading edge of a movement without help from establishment or mainstream publishers or producers.

venue – a place where specific kinds of events take place.

Web Sites

To learn more about cool music, visit ABDO Publishing Company on the World Wide Web at **www.abdopublishing.com**. Web sites about cool music are featured on our Book Links pages. These links are routinely monitored and updated to provide the most current

Index